THROUGH ARTISTS' EYES

Society & Class

Jane Bingham

www.raintreepublishers.co.uk
Visit our website to find out more information about **Raintree** books.

To order:
☎ Phone 44 (0) 1865 888113
🖹 Send a fax to 44 (0) 1865 314091
💻 Visit the Raintree bookshop at **www.raintreepublishers.co.uk** to browse our catalogue and order online.

First published in Great Britain by Raintree,
Halley Court, Jordan Hill, Oxford OX2 8EJ,
part of Harcourt Education.

Raintree is a registered trademark of Harcourt Education Ltd.

Editorial: Isabel Thomas and Rosie Gordon
Design: Richard Parker & Tinstar Design www.tinstar.com
Picture Research: Hannah Taylor and Zoe Spilberg
Production: Duncan Gilbert

Originated by Chroma Graphics
Printed and bound in China by South China Printing Company

10-digit ISBN 1 406 20150 2
13-digit ISBN 978 1 4062 0150 5

10 09 08 07 06
10 9 8 7 6 5 4 3 2 1

British Library Cataloguing in Publication Data
Bingham, Jane
  Society and class. - (Through artists' eyes)
  1.Society in art - Juvenile literature 2.Social classes in art - Juvenile literature 3.Art - History - Juvenile literature
  I.Title
        704'.0862

The publishers would like to thank Karen Hosack for her assistance in the preparation of this book.

Acknowledgements
The publishers would like to thank the following for permission to reproduce photographs: **p. 31**, © 1990, Photo Scala, Florence/ Hermitage Museum, St Petersburg; **p. 42**, © DACS 2006 Photo: Bridgeman Art Library/ Akademie der Kunst, Berlin, Germany, Alinari; **p. 44**, © DACS 2006 Photo: Bridgeman Art Library/ State Art Museum, Samara; **p. 48**, © The Andy Warhol Foundation for the Visual Arts, Inc./ ARS, NY and Dacs, London 2006 Photo: © 2000. Photo The Andy Warhol Foundation/ Art Resource/ Scala, Florence; **p. 50**, © The George and Helen Segal Foundation/ DACS, London/ VAGA, New York 2006 Photo: 2005. Digital Image, The Museum of Modern Art, New York/ Scala, Florence; **p. 51**, © Tom Hunter. Courtesy Jay Jopling/ White Cube (London); **p. 20**, Ancient Art and Architecture Collection Ltd/ Ronald Sheridan; **p. 26**, Bodleian Library, Oxford; Bridgeman Art Library, **pp. 47; 32**, (Metropolitan Museum of Art, New York, USA), **27**, (Rafael Valls Gallery, London, UK), **17**, (© Walker Art Gallery, National Museum Liverpool), **29**, (© Worcester Art Museum, Massachusetts, USA), **21**, (Bibliotheque Nationale, Paris, France, Lauros / Giraudon), **37**, (Capitol Collection, Washington, USA), **9**, (Egyptian National Museum, Cairo, Egypt), **25**, (Musee Conde, Chantilly, France), **22**, (Musee Conde, Chantilly, France, Giraudon), **19**, (Musee de l'Armee, Paris, France, Giraudon), **4**, (Musee d'Orsay, Paris, France, Giraudon), **33**, (National Gallery of Art, Washington DC, USA), **28, 41**, (National Gallery, London, UK), **13**, (National Museum of India, New Delhi, India), **23**, (Private Collection), **35**, (Private Collection), **45**, (Private Collection), **46**, (Private Collection), **49**, (Private Collection, © Bonhams, London, UK), **15**, (Private Collection, Archives Charmet), **30**, (Rijksmuseum, Amsterdam, Holland), **11**, (San Vitale, Ravenna, Italy, Giraudon); **p.39**, Coming from the Mill 1930 © The Lowry Collection, Salford; **p. 34**, Corbis/ Bettmann; **p. 14**, Corbis/ Werner Forman Archive; **p. 43**, Magnum/ Henri Cartier-Bresson; The Art Archive **pp. 18** (Dagli Orti), **12**, (John Webb), **6**, (Musée des Antiquités St Germain en Laye / Dagli Orti), **36, 40** (Musée d'Orsay, Paris/ Dagli/ Orti).
Cover image: Guy Pene Du Bois (American 1884-1958) "Café D'Harcourt" circa 1905-6 reproduced courtesy of The Estate of Guy Pene du Bois and James Graham & Sons, New York.

Contents

Any words that appear in bold, **like this**, are explained in the glossary.

Introduction

At first sight, it looks like a peaceful country scene – three women working in a field at the end of a golden summer's day. But take a second look at the painting. Is it really a happy scene? Why do the women have to bend almost double? And what exactly are they gathering?

When you look carefully at *The Gleaners*, you can see that the three **peasant** women have managed to gather almost nothing at all. This is because the crop has already been harvested. (You can see the corn stacked up in the distance beside the houses of the wealthy farmers.) Meanwhile, all that is left for the poor are the few stalks of corn that they can "glean".

Jean-François Millet's *The Gleaners* (1857). Millet has made the three women gleaners look very graceful – even though they are doing a miserable job. Why do you think he chose to make the gleaners look beautiful?

In his painting *The Gleaners* the artist, Jean-François Millet, was making a passionate protest. Millet came from a poor peasant family and he was very angry at the way that people of his class were treated. Through his work, he wanted to open people's eyes to the unfairness of society. "This is what life is like for the poor," Millet says through his painting. "They have to work so hard just to survive, while the rich have more than they need."

Society through artists' eyes

Throughout history, artists have observed the people around them. They have painted images of people doing different jobs and playing different roles in society. Some of these images were produced for rich and powerful figures, and these works often show society through the eyes of those wealthy people.

In other works of art, artists reveal their personal response to the world in which they live. Works like Millet's *The Gleaners* express a clear criticism of society.

A range of art

This book starts with **prehistoric** cave paintings and ends in the 21st century. It ranges across the world, and covers paintings and sculptures, and also literature. To help you to see exactly where a work of art was made, there is a map of the world on page 52. The timeline on page 53 provides an overview of the different periods of history discussed in the book.

For thousands of years, artists have been putting up a mirror to our society. Through their images, we can see the way that people of different classes have lived, and how they have related to other people in society.

What is society?

Society is all the people who live in a country or area. People in society come from different classes and all of them have different roles to play. They can range from rulers to farmers or shopkeepers, but all of them are equally necessary to make up society.

In a successful society, people from all classes feel pleased to belong to their community. They feel that they are working together to make their society work well. However, societies do not always work smoothly and different classes can feel unfairly treated.

Early hunters and farmers

Around 30,000 years ago, people in southern Europe began to paint on the walls of the caves where they lived. These early artists pictured their way of life – painting figures of hunters, armed with spears, chasing after large animals, such as bison and wild deer. The prehistoric cave paintings show how human society began, with people making simple tools and hunting animals for food.

Prehistoric cave paintings such as these from Lascaux, France, c.1500 BCE, provide valuable clues about our distant ancestors' way of life. The paintings show that prehistoric people lived by hunting, but some of them were also artists.

Chiefs and hunters

Around 16,000 years ago, some cave dwellers in Altamira in northern Spain created a series of painted scenes. These striking images show hunters chasing after animals and also show the hunters performing a **ritual** dance. Led by their chief, the hunters take giant leaps, waving their bows and arrows over their heads. The hunters wear feathers in their hair, but the chief has a taller headdress. These paintings show that early hunting societies were organized into groups with a leader. They also show that the early people performed religious rituals.

Early farmers

Around 10,000 BCE, some people in the Middle East discovered how to grow crops. This knowledge gradually spread to India and North Africa. People slowly stopped their hunting way of life and became farmers, living in villages.

A tomb painting from Ancient Egypt gives a clear image of early farming life. A farmer uses one hand to guide his wooden plough, and holds up a rattle to scare away the birds in his other hand. Behind him, a woman follows the plough, scattering seed from a bag.

The painting shows that both men and women worked together on the land. It also suggests that a farmer's life was a tough one – as the hard-working farmer bent over his plough has to perform two tasks at once.

Hunter-gatherers of Australia

Most prehistoric people survived by a mixture of hunting animals and gathering food. However, when people discovered how to grow crops, the hunter-gatherer way of life disappeared in most parts of the world. This did not happen in the dry, desert land of Australia. Here, the **Aboriginal people** continued their traditional hunter-gathering way of life for thousands of years. They also continued to paint on rocks. Aboriginal rock paintings show hunters with spears. They also show people with "dilly bags" woven from reeds. These bags are used for gathering fruits and seeds.

Mighty rulers

Around 2000 BCE, powerful leaders began to build up kingdoms in the Middle East. These rulers were treated like gods by their people. They dressed in splendid clothes and lived an incredibly luxurious life, waited on by servants. Several images of these early rulers have survived.

Assyrian kings

The ancient Assyrian kings ruled over an empire based in present-day northern-Iraq and southeastern Turkey. They gave themselves titles such as "King of the Universe" and had some astonishing palaces and gardens built for them.

Some carvings survive showing King Ashurnasipal II of Assyria in his palace. One servant holds a parasol over the king's head, while another writes down everything the king says. Another carving shows the king and queen relaxing in their garden. The king lies on a couch, and by his side is a table, laden with figs and grapes. Servants stand behind the king and queen, cooling them with fans.

Another servant brings a tray of cakes, while three musicians play for the royal couple. The carvings reveal that the Assyrian king and queen had incredible power, while their servants had to devote their lives to looking after all the royal couple's needs.

Egyptian pharaohs

The rulers of the Egyptian empire were known as "**pharaohs**". They were treated like gods during their lifetime and buried in massive pyramids after their death. Larger-than-life carvings of the pharaohs are often found on the walls of temples and palaces. These imposing images show the pharaohs staring straight ahead, carrying their symbols of power, such as a curved staff, known as a crook, and a flail (or whip).

We know that the carvings of the pharaohs were made at the command of the later pharaohs. They were clearly meant to impress the ordinary Egyptian people with the great power of their rulers.

Bearded queen

At one stage in Egypt's history, there was no male successor to the Egyptian throne, so a pharaoh's daughter, called Hatshepsut, became pharaoh. Several Egyptian artists show her dressed exactly like a male pharaoh, wearing a headdress and a false beard.

Egyptian paintings show that the ordinary farmers and soldiers dressed very differently from the pharaoh. While most Egyptian men wore simple tunics, and had short, loose hair, and no beard, the pharaoh wore an elaborate headdress, heavy eye make-up, and a long, plaited beard. This made the pharaoh look entirely different from anybody else in his kingdom.

The golden mummy case of the Egyptian pharaoh Tutankhamun was made around 1320 BCE. It shows an idealized image of the young ruler. However, it is much more than just a portrait. By its use of precious materials and its inclusion of magical symbols (such as the serpent and the vulture) it presents the pharaoh as a **divine** being. The artist is saying that here is a god who should be worshipped by his people.

Roman rulers

For 500 years, the mighty Roman Empire was ruled by a series of all-powerful emperors. It was very important that all the people in the Empire were loyal to their emperor, and one of the best ways to make the emperor known throughout the Empire was to create striking images of him.

Coins showing the emperor's head were used all over the Roman Empire. Also, many statues were put in public places. These statues **portrayed** the emperors as handsome heroes, in order to inspire public loyalty.

Augustus was the first Roman emperor. He ruled from 27 BCE to 14 CE, and won many new lands for the Empire in battle. During his reign (time as leader), coins were issued showing a side view of Augustus with a crown of laurel leaves in his hair. The laurel crown showed his authority. In profile, Augustus was instantly recognizable. After this, all Roman emperors were portrayed on coins in this way.

Byzantine rulers

In 476 CE, the Roman Empire in the west collapsed, but the Empire in the east continued for another thousand years. It became known as the "Byzantine Empire", and its emperors aimed to be as powerful and respected as the Roman Emperors had been. One of the greatest Byzantine emperors was Justinian, in the 6th century CE.

He conquered many lands that had once belonged to the Roman Empire in the west.

Justinian's success as a ruler was largely due to his remarkable wife, the Empress Theodora. She helped him to create a great Christian Empire with a totally new system of laws. Theodora encouraged lawyers, priests, **merchants**, and artists to visit their great palace at Constantinople (present-day Istanbul).

A ruling couple

After Justinian conquered Italy, he and Theodora **commissioned** an artist to create a set of stunning **mosaics** for the cathedral in Ravenna. The mosaics include two scenes. One shows Justinian with his priests and ministers, and the other portrays Theodora with her **ladies-in-waiting** and her advisors. At that time, it was very unusual for an emperor to recognize the importance of his wife, and this is one of the first known images of a ruling couple.

Augustus the conqueror

Several statues of Augustus have survived and all of them show the emperor as a strong and commanding figure. One famous statue shows Augustus dressed in his army general's uniform, with one arm raised as if he is urging his troops on to victory. This inspiring sculpture was clearly supposed to make the Roman people feel confident and optimistic.

A mosaic portrait of the Byzantine Empress Theodora from Ravenna in Italy. This imposing portrait, which was made around 540 CE, emphasizes Theodora's power. The empress wears an impressive crown and robes, and the artist has even given her a halo, as if she were a Christian saint. Theodora's husband, the Emperor Justinian, is also shown at Ravenna, but the artist presents Theodora as equally important to her husband. This was very unusual at the time.

Caliphs and sultans

In the 8th century CE, the followers of the **prophet Mohammed** built up a vast Arab Empire. The Empire was ruled from Baghdad by a powerful ruler, known as the "caliph". Persian artists painted miniature portraits of the caliph in his palace. Some of these paintings show the rulers feasting, attended by beautiful serving girls. Others show them enjoying a bath or a massage. These works of art show the kind of luxury and privilege that the caliphs enjoyed. They also show how women could be treated in this society.

The Arab Empire lasted for over 500 years, but then the Turks took control of Baghdad. The Turkish rulers were known as "sultans". They enjoyed a luxurious lifestyle, but they were also fierce warriors. The sultans paid skilful artists to paint their portraits. These paintings show the bearded sultans dressed in turbans and flowing, colourful robes, staring straight ahead without smiling. The paintings send out a message that these are rulers to be respected and feared.

An early explorer's map, showing the **Islamic** king Mansa Musa, who ruled over the North African kingdom of Mali, being visited by a merchant. He was very rich, and he is shown here holding a golden coin. Because the mapmaker was from Europe, he has made Mansa Musa look like a European king.

Mogul emperors

In 1526, a group of Arabs known as the Moguls invaded India. The Moguls ruled northern India for the next 300 years and introduced many artistic traditions from the Arab Empire. Mogul emperors paid for magnificent **mosques** and palaces to be built, including the exquisite Taj Mahal. They also commissioned artists to create delicate paintings, **ceramics**, **textiles**, and metalwork.

Mogul artists painted miniature scenes showing the lives of the emperors. Some of these paintings show the emperors enjoying their leisure time, riding on elephants, or hunting with hawks. Other paintings show military triumphs, weddings, and other celebrations. The scenes are packed with tiny figures, such as soldiers, **courtiers**, dancers, and musicians.

One famous Mogul miniature painting gives us some idea of the extent of the Mogul emperors' riches. It **depicts** the annual birthday ceremony in which the emperor was weighed against a pan full of gold, silver, and other valuables taken from the royal treasury. These treasures were then given to good causes.

The miniature paintings show Mogul rulers' amazing wealth and power, and this is the impression that their artists were paid to give. However, it is possible to see these scenes in a very different way.

Did everyone in the Mogul court enjoy their work? How would it feel to spend your life serving an emperor who was so astonishingly rich?

In this 15th-century miniature, the first Mogul emperor, Babur, holds a hawk, and is surrounded by servants, guards, and people asking advice. The artist shows the emperor as powerful, rich, handsome, and wise.

African rulers

From the 13th to the 19th century, Benin in western Africa was ruled by powerful kings. They were known as "obas". The obas encouraged local craftworkers to create beautiful artworks for the royal palace. By the 15th century, the **sculptors** of Benin were making exquisite portrait heads, figures, and animals. All of these sculptures were made from bronze or brass. The Benin portrait heads represented the oba, his family, and his **ancestors**. These heads were placed on palace altars, where they were worshipped as gods.

Some of the surviving heads show the oba wearing a crown. Many others portray the oba's mother, known as the "iyoba".

The iyoba, or queen mother, had a very important role in Benin society. She advised her son, acting as a wise, mother-goddess figure. The sculptures of the iyobas show elegant, powerful women, staring ahead, with large eyes and delicate features. Often the queen mother wears a high collar of beads around her neck and a tall pointed crown. All the portrait sculptures have a sense of dignity.

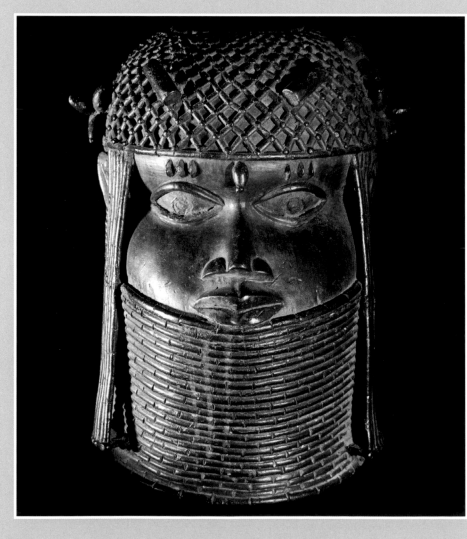

A bronze head from Benin showing a powerful queen mother, or iyoba. The queen's high position in society is indicated by her jewellery – a high beaded necklace and an elaborate headdress.

14

Chinese emperors

China was ruled by emperors from the 3rd century BCE until the early 20th century. The Chinese believed their emperors were divine, so they were waited on hand and foot. A painting of the Emperor Taizong, who ruled in the 7th century CE, shows him seated on a stool carried by four court ladies. Two more carry huge fans to keep the emperor cool, while another holds up a banner behind him. None of the ladies looks at the emperor because it was strictly forbidden to see his face. The painting shows the power of the emperor, but also the way that women were treated in ancient Chinese society.

Many portraits of Chinese emperors show them seated on ornate thrones, wearing **embroidered** robes, and staring straight ahead.

The official portrait of the Emperor Kangxi, who ruled from 1661 to 1722, pictures him sitting stiffly in an elaborate robe, with long sleeves that cover the emperor's hands, indicating that he does no work. European paintings of the same period show wealthy gentlemen with full sleeves and lacy cuffs. They give the same message – that this person is too grand to work with their hands.

This painting shows the Chinese emperor and empress with their court. The emperor and his wife sit on thrones surrounded by their ladies-in-waiting and servants. Meanwhile, the ordinary people are hard at work.

Imperial yellow

The Chinese emperor's official robes were yellow. This was the imperial (royal) colour that only the emperor and his family could wear. The china used to serve the emperor's food was also yellow.

Medieval rulers

During the **Middle Ages**, the countries of Europe were ruled by emperors, kings, and queens. People were taught that their rulers were chosen by God, and that these rulers had a **divine right** to rule over their subjects. **Medieval** rulers employed artists and sculptors to reflect this view.

Most medieval portraits of rulers show kings and queens dressed in their royal robes and carrying their symbols of office, such as a golden "orb", representing the world, and a jewelled staff, known as a "sceptre". However, while lots of attention is paid to the royal robes, most of the faces show very little character. This is not simply a matter of lack of skill. While a few artists attempted to show the true character of the individual **monarchs**, most of them were content simply to present what the rulers wanted their subjects to see – an image of a perfect, God-given ruler.

Tudor monarchs

By the 16th century, artists had begun to show their kings and queens as instantly recognizable individuals. In particular, Hans Holbein's portraits of King Henry VIII of England reveal a man of very strong character. Holbein's most famous portrait shows the king with his legs planted wide apart in a confident and aggressive pose. Although Henry does not wear his royal crown, there is no doubting his wealth and power. He is richly dressed in fine **brocades** and holds his hands clenched, as if ready for action. One hand is dangerously close to his dagger, while in his other hand he holds a glove, as if he is preparing to throw it down in a challenge. The portrait sends out a very clear warning that here is a man who must be obeyed.

Henry VIII's daughter, Queen Elizabeth I, knew the importance of presenting a powerful public image. During her long reign, she **commissioned** a number of talented artists to paint her portrait. In each of these paintings, Elizabeth is exquisitely dressed and perfectly made-up with a pale, doll-like face. She appears to be an almost **supernatural** creature. This was an effect Elizabeth deliberately created, and she liked to be known as the "Faerie Queen".

The Armada portrait

In 1588, Queen Elizabeth's navy defeated a huge fleet of ships called the Spanish Armada and prevented the Spanish king from invading England. To mark this important victory, Elizabeth had her portrait painted. The painting shows the victorious queen resting her hand on a globe, clearly wanting to show that she has control of the world's oceans.

King Henry VIII of England, painted by Hans Holbein the Younger around 1537. The portrait emphasizes Henry's physical size and strength. The king's pose, with his legs wide apart, was very unusual for a portrait at this time. However, in medieval paintings, Saint George was usually shown standing like this after slaying the dragon. So Holbein may have been deliberately comparing Henry with the brave patron saint of England.

The "Sun King" and the Emperor

Many rulers have used the power of art to create a strong public image for themselves. But two figures stand out in the history of France – one was King Louis XIV and the other was the Emperor Napoleon Bonaparte.

Louis XIV ruled France from 1643 to 1715. Early in his reign, he acted the part of the sun in a play, and after that he was often known as the "Sun King". Louis was a very showy monarch who built a huge palace at Versailles, surrounded by spectacular gardens. Images of the king were placed all over the palace and its grounds. Apart from many paintings depicting Louis as a dashing young hero, there were also dozens of carvings of his face surrounded by sunbeams. In these golden carvings, Louis appeared like a god of the sun. Through the power of art, Louis made himself almost godlike.

At the start of the 19th century, Napoleon Bonaparte won some brilliant military victories for France. Since the French Revolution, the country no longer had a king (see pages 36–37). However, Napoleon wanted to rule over all the people he had conquered, just like the Roman emperors had done.

Golden badges like this, showing the Sun King, are found all over the palace and gardens of Versailles. The two crossed rods are symbols of French royal power.

In 1804, Napoleon was crowned Emperor of France in a spectacular ceremony (called a "coronation"). After this, Napoleon commissioned France's leading artists to paint his portrait in his robes.

One of the most famous portraits of the Emperor was painted by J. A. D. Ingres. This impressive work shows the Emperor seated on a throne. He holds a golden staff in his hand and a second staff and a sword rest at his side, while his foot is placed on a gilded cushion – all clear symbols of the Emperor's strength and power. On his head is a golden crown of laurel leaves, a deliberate copy of the crown of the Roman emperors.

Images of royalty

By the end of the 19th century, most countries no longer had a **monarchy**. However, a few nations still kept their kings and queens. Today's kings and queens have very little power, but they still have an important role to play as the nation's **figurehead**. Figureheads need to be instantly recognized, so many images of them are produced. The head of the British queen appears on national stamps and coins. Members of the royal families still pose for painters and photographers, but these new images are much more relaxed and **informal** than the portraits of the past. This deliberate change of image shows the changing character of royalty today.

Ingres also created a golden glow around the Emperor, as though he were a god. In this painting, Napoleon is transformed. He is no longer a simple soldier, but becomes an almost divine being.

J. A. D. Ingres, *Napoleon on his Imperial Throne* (1806). Ingres' portrait presents a sense of power. Even the designs on the carpet below the Emperor's feet show Napoleon's role as conqueror and ruler.

Slaves, serfs, and soldiers

The ancient societies of Egypt, Greece, and Rome all relied on slaves to keep them running smoothly. Slaves belonged entirely to their master or mistress and had no rights at all. Often, they had been captured and taken far away from their own people. They had no freedom to choose where they lived or how they spent their lives. They could only marry other slaves and their children were also slaves. It was a desperate existence and some brave slaves tried to free themselves.

Artists and slaves

Artists often included images of slaves in their pictures of life in the ancient world. These images reveal clear differences in the ways that masters and slaves dressed. However, only a few works of art show slaves as real individuals, and almost none of them give any idea of how it felt to be a slave. In some ways this seems strange as many artists were slaves themselves. However, the artists were probably much too afraid of their master's anger to show any sympathy for their fellow slaves.

Egyptian slaves

In Ancient Egypt, the pharaohs used armies of slaves to build their magnificent temples and pyramids, but these hard-working people are almost never shown in Egyptian art. The pharaohs also kept household slaves to look after them and their families, and to cook and serve their food. One Egyptian **fresco** shows slaves working hard at a banquet. Some are serving the pharaoh and his guests with food, while others are placing cones of scented fat on the female guests' heads as a way to cool them down. The contrast between the slaves' simple **loincloths** and the guests' fine clothes is very clear.

Roman slaves

The Romans relied on slaves to keep their empire running. Many slaves had to join the army or navy (see page 21) while others were forced to do very dangerous work in mines or building sites. Roman carvings show slaves building a temple, working on a treadmill, and climbing rickety scaffolding. Other works of art show slaves working in shops and workshops, or in private homes, helping their mistresses to dress, cooking, cleaning, and serving meals.

A fresco from Pompeii, showing a Roman lady with a slave helping with her hair.

Soldier slaves

The Islamic rulers of the Ottoman Empire used soldier slaves to help them win their victories. The Ottomans captured boys from Christian parts of their empire and trained them to be expert soldiers, known as "janissaries". The janissaries feature in several Ottoman paintings of battles and processions. They stand out because of their distinctive costume of tall pointed hats.

A **manuscript** painting showing Ottoman janissaries – warrior slaves who were forced to fight for the Turkish Ottoman emperors. The janissaries belonged to the Ottoman emperor. They had to follow very strict rules and were not allowed to marry.

Medieval serfs

By the start of the Middle Ages, rulers in Europe no longer kept slaves. However, this did not mean that everyone was free. Most ordinary people worked on the land, which was owned by wealthy landowners. These poor workers, known as **serfs**, had to swear loyalty to their lord, and they were not allowed to leave his land. In return for their work on his land, the lord allowed his serfs to keep some food for their own families. The lord also gave his serfs protection in times of war, offering them shelter inside his castle.

Serfs and lords

One of the best visual records of the relationship between a rich nobleman and his serfs is provided by a medieval prayer book. *The Duke of Berry's Book of Hours* belonged to a 15th century French **noble**. It includes a beautifully illustrated calendar, showing activities for each month of the year. Some of the scenes show the serfs working in the fields, with the Duke's castle rising in the background. Others show the Duke and his guests feasting or hunting, waited on by their loyal servants. In these detailed paintings of medieval life, the dramatic contrast between the lifestyles of the lord and his serfs seems very clear. However, the calendar's artists were simply painting country life as they knew it.

A spring scene from *The Duke of Berry's Book of Hours*. The peasants in the foreground are shabbily dressed, and working very hard. Meanwhile, in the background, the Duke's magnificent castle stretches over the hillside.

Bruegel's paintings provide a fascinating view of everyday life in 16th-century Holland. Bruegel was one of the earliest artists to concentrate on the lives of the ordinary people.

Bruegel's peasants

The 16th-century artist Pieter Bruegel the Elder painted many scenes of peasant life. He shows country people working hard in the fields, but also having fun – feasting, dancing, and playing games. One of his best-known images is *The Peasant Wedding*, which shows a celebration held in a barn involving simple country people of all ages.

Bruegel dressed as a peasant in order to join in the farmers' daily lives. His paintings of peasant life seem much more accurate than the work of other artists of his time, who tended to show peasants simply as rough and drunken fools. However, he was a learned city-dweller and his paintings were produced for educated, **sophisticated** people.

The Peasant Wedding does not just show a simple country celebration. It also contains many examples of foolish human nature. The bride seems stupidly happy and many of the characters indulge in greedy and foolish behaviour. All of these examples are intended to make the thoughtful viewer think carefully about the many weaknesses of human nature. However, even though Bruegel uses the peasant scene to teach lessons about human behaviour, he does not seem deliberately scornful or cruel towards the peasant people. Instead he portrays his peasant characters in a gentle, affectionate way.

Ancient warriors

The rulers of the ancient world all relied on vast armies of soldiers. These soldiers were often slaves or prisoners of war who were forced to spend their lives fighting incredibly dangerous wars.

Artists produced many images of these warriors. They show soldiers marching to war and in the thick of battle. They also show images of triumphant armies returning home. These images were intended to reassure and encourage the people at home and fill them with pride in their army. They do very little to reveal the negative side of the soldiers' lives.

Early armies

Around 2500 BCE, artists from Ancient Sumeria, the world's first known civilization, created a work of art known as the "Standard of Ur". The Standard was a kind of banner that was probably carried in processions. On one side it shows scenes of farming life, while on the other it shows the Sumerian army marching to war, riding in war chariots, and fighting a battle. Clearly, soldiers already had a very important role to play in society.

Roman soldiers

The Roman emperors built massive monuments to celebrate their military victories, and covered these columns and arches with carvings of soldiers. Roman soldiers are shown as brave, determined, and loyal, while their leaders are shown as splendid heroes.

It was very important for the Roman emperors and generals to have complete loyalty and obedience from all parts of their society. One excellent way to gain this loyalty was through art. They paid artists to create inspiring images of heroic leaders, followed into battle by their unquestioning men.

Medieval knights

In medieval Europe, a new type of soldier emerged. Medieval **knights** were highly skilled warriors who rode on horseback. They trained for years in the art of fighting, dressed in elaborate armour, and carried shields with their own **coat of arms**.

In the Middle Ages, the knight was a glamorous hero. Poets told of the amazing adventures of famous knights, and artists produced colourful images of knights in battle. Skilled carvers also carved impressive **effigies** on the tombs of dead knights. All these works of art helped to create the myth of the perfect warrior.

Later soldiers

After the Middle Ages, a new kind of soldier emerged in Europe. Soldiers fought in large national armies. They stopped wearing armour and wore easily recognizable uniforms. Artists continued to show images of battles, but most of these images did not concentrate on individual soldiers. Instead, they glorified the role of the armies' leaders.

By the 20th century, there had been a change in the way that artists saw the role of the ordinary soldier. Artists began to show the soldiers as suffering human beings, caught up in the horror of war. Some powerful paintings, poems, and photographs reveal the terrible experiences of the men and women who fought in the two World Wars, and in other conflicts since then.

This medieval manuscript painting shows three knights leaving a tournament (contest). Knights were respected figures in medieval society. As well as being skilled soldiers, they had to follow strict rules of polite behaviour.

Craftworkers, traders, and merchants

By the 12th century, some people in medieval Europe were living in towns. Town dwellers were mainly craftworkers and shopkeepers, but merchants also used the towns as their base for trading and selling goods.

Many towns grew up on the coast or on the banks of wide rivers. These towns could easily be reached by merchant ships and they became important centres for trade. They also became centres for crafts and art. Craftworkers and artists working in the towns could buy a range of materials from distant lands, such as precious metals, gems, and dyes. Artists also found plenty of opportunities to sell their work in the growing cities and towns.

Images of towns

Medieval artists have left some detailed images of the towns and ports where they lived. These pictures show lively, bustling places, with workshops and houses packed tightly together around a central square.

One of the best-known images of a medieval town shows the famous merchant and explorer Marco Polo setting off on his travels. In this 15th-century manuscript painting, a group of richly dressed merchants gather on the quay at the port of Venice. The city of Venice is represented as a crowded jumble of fine buildings and bridges.

A 15th-century manuscript painting showing Marco Polo preparing to leave Venice. The painting provides a fascinating view of city life in the late Middle Ages.

Other **citizens** go about their business, carrying jugs and bundles, selling their wares, and meeting their friends. Meanwhile, the harbour is filled with boats and ships of all sizes. In the medieval artist's eyes, Venice seems to be a cheerful and wealthy place.

Images of townspeople

Medieval manuscripts contain many images of townspeople at work. These images provide a fascinating glimpse into the working lives of ordinary men and women, as butchers, bakers, shoemakers, and potters are all shown hard at work in their shops and workshops.

A few surviving images show medieval artists, standing at their easels with their pots of paint arranged by their side. They may be early examples of self-portraits.

Some paintings show female artists, but these are rare. The role of most women in the Middle Ages was to support their husband by running the home and caring for the children.

Portraits of merchants

By the 15th century, wealthy merchants were paying artists to paint their portraits. Many portraits of merchants dressed in their finest clothes have survived. Often, the merchant poses alone, but sometimes they are accompanied by their wife and children. The main purpose of these paintings was to show off the wealth and power of the merchants. If the merchant sold cloth, the paintings were a fine chance to show off his wares, modelled by his family!

Cornelis Verbeeck *A Dutch Merchant ship off a rocky coast* (c.1590–1635). This painting shows merchant ships on a stormy sea, sailing past craggy rocks. Wealthy merchants often commissioned paintings to show off their ships and also to show the risks they took at sea.

Masters and servants

After the Middle Ages, most lords and nobles no longer lived in castles, but that did not mean the end of the nobility. Members of the upper class in Europe and North America continued to enjoy a grand and luxurious lifestyle. They lived in large houses, surrounded by extensive grounds. They dressed in fine clothes and had plenty of leisure time. Meanwhile, vast numbers of people worked as servants for the **aristocracy**, looking after all their needs.

Art for aristocrats

Many members of the aristocracy commissioned artists to produce lavish portraits of their families.

These "society portraits" were often set against a background of the family home or grounds. The paintings provide a fascinating view of the lifestyle and attitudes of the ruling classes.

Thomas Gainsborough

The British painter Thomas Gainsborough was a leading portrait artist in the 18th century. He began his career by painting merchants but then moved on to portraits of the aristocracy.

One of Gainsborough's most famous paintings, *Mr and Mrs Andrews*, shows a recently married couple who both came from very wealthy families.

Thomas Gainsborough, *Mr and Mrs Andrews* (c. 1750). The newly married couple pose stiffly in front of their country estate. One of the main aims of the portrait seems to be to show off the couple's land.

The couple are posed under a tree, with a view of their estate in the background. The figure of Mr Andrews suggests power and authority, as he leans casually against a garden seat with his gun under his arm, and his dog gazing up obediently. Meanwhile, Mrs Andrews sits stiffly upright, with her beautiful dress draped carefully over the seat, as if to avoid dirtying it by contact with the ground. The portrait is dominated by the couple's land and so it appears to be a portrait of the joining of two country estates, rather than a picture of a love match.

John Singer Sargent

The US painter John Singer Sargent made his reputation by painting grand members of society around the beginning of the 20th century. Sargent specialized in painting beautiful women and successful men, wearing elegant evening dress.

In Sargent's portrait of Lady Agnew of Lochnaugh, the artist shows a rich and beautiful young woman wearing an exquisite dress with delicate, transparent sleeves. The young woman sits back comfortably in an elegant chair against a background of fine Chinese wallpaper. Sargent lovingly paints all these different **textiles**, to give us a sense of the comfort and glamour of Lady Agnew's life. He also manages to show through these details that she is a woman of up-to-date and **sophisticated** tastes.

John Singer Sargent, *Lady Warwick and her Son* (1905). Sargent painted this picture to fit in with Lady Warwick's older family portraits. It follows the style of 18th-century artists such as Gainsborough. Lady Warwick and her son, in their finest clothes, are shown in the family estate. The picture seems posed and false, and there is little sense of closeness between mother and son.

Paintings of servants

Until the start of the 20th century, large numbers of people in Europe worked as servants. In particular, women worked as cooks and maidservants, preparing all the meals for the household, doing the shopping, and keeping the house clean. Many portrait painters concentrated on showing society figures and simply ignored the servant classes. However, in the 17th century, a group of painters in the Netherlands turned their attention to the lives of domestic servants.

The Dutch painters chose to show domestic scenes because they were painting for a different kind of audience. Dutch paintings were much smaller than the society portraits being painted in other parts of Europe. This shows that the pictures could be bought by a wider group of people, especially **middle class** merchants. Merchants preferred to have homely images in their houses. However, the pictures of perfect domestic calm that many artists portrayed were not completely true to life. They showed a romantic picture of domestic bliss that the busy merchants longed for.

Vermeer and de Hooch

Several Dutch painters produced portraits of serving girls and women, some absorbed in their work, and others sitting to have their portraits taken. The most famous of these images is Jan Vermeer's *The Milkmaid,*

which shows a serving girl pouring milk by a window. The girl is stockily built and plainly dressed but she has a powerful sense of dignity and calm as she goes about her daily work.

Jan Vermeer, *The Milkmaid* (1558–1560). Vermeer shows a plainly dressed serving girl absorbed in her work. Up until this time, very few artists thought that servants were interesting subjects for art.

Another Dutch master, Pieter de Hooch, included many images of serving women in his paintings. De Hooch's serving women are often old and plain and go about their business patiently, while their masters and mistresses enjoy their leisure. One painting, *A Young Man's Morning*, tells a clear story. A half-dressed young man lounges on a chair, while behind him a bent old woman is making his bed. Even though we cannot see the servant's face, the message of the painting is clear. Some lucky members of society are born to a life of leisure, while others are forced to work hard, even when they are old. Peter de Hooch came from a poor family and worked as a servant for a while. His paintings show his respect for the hardworking, honest people whose job was to serve others.

Michiel Sweerts

Michiel Sweerts was working at the same time as Vermeer and de Hooch. He produced some powerful portraits of serving girls and women. His portrait of *A Young Maidservant*, painted in 1660, shows a teenage girl in a drab brown dress. The girl has a long, wistful face and she looks away from the painter with an expression of sadness and longing. Another portrait by Sweerts shows *An Old Woman Spinning*. Her ragged clothing is in holes, and her face is lined and worn. The woman gazes straight ahead with a dull hopeless stare, as if she feels defeated by the harshness of her life.

Pieter de Hooch painted *A Mistress and her Maid* in the 1660s. The mistress of the house seems to be inspecting a pan that the maid has cleaned. Many of de Hooch's paintings show merchants' wives, running their homes with the help of their servants.

Settlers in a new land

In the 1650s, boatloads of settlers from Europe began to arrive in North America. Over the next 200 years, the settlers gradually spread out across the continent, claiming the land as their own. Artists recorded the lives of the settlers and also painted images of the Native Americans. Many of these images showed a very romantic and one-sided view of the settlers as brave **pioneers**, facing hostile attacks from the native people.

American settlers

A very famous painter of American settlers was George Caleb Bingham, who worked in the mid-19th century.

Bingham painted peaceful scenes of everyday life in the American West, set against a background of spectacular scenery. He also created dramatic compositions, showing brave pioneers travelling westward to find new land.

In *Fur Traders Descending the Missouri*, Bingham shows a father and son rowing down a vast river in the misty sunlight. The trader's young son leans on a chest filled with furs to sell, while a black bear cub on a lead sits in the prow of the boat. The painting shows the loneliness of the settlers' life but also their spirit of adventure.

George Caleb Bingham, *Fur Traders Descending the Missouri (1845)*. Bingham was a self-taught artist, who worked on the family farm for many years before he became a full-time painter. His paintings often present a rather romantic, idealized view of the settlers' life.

Another painting by Bingham shows the famous pioneer Daniel Boone escorting a group of settlers through a dangerous mountain path. Boone walks ahead with gun at the ready, leading a woman mounted on a horse. All around the group is dark and menacing scenery.

Portraits of Native Americans

While Bingham was producing his romantic paintings of settlers, another artist was concentrating on painting the Native American people. George Catlin produced hundreds of studies of the people of the Missouri plains, including portraits of individual chiefs, paintings of ceremonies, and scenes from everyday life, such as hunting and fishing.

Catlin realized that the Native American way of life was rapidly vanishing and tried to produce a true picture of what he saw. However, many other artists produced very inaccurate images of Native Americans. They did not take the trouble to observe the native tribes' real behaviour or appearance, and the coarse images that they created helped to continue myths of "wild" and "primitive" "savages".

Settlers in Australia

From the 1780s onwards, settlers from Europe began to take over Australia. They fought many battles for land with the Aboriginal people. At the time, these battles were recorded by European artists. Recently, however, some Aboriginal artists have produced some very different pictures of the conflict. In particular, Harry J. Wedge has painted some shocking images of **massacres** by the early settlers.

George Catlin, *White Cloud, head chief of the Iowas* (1844–1845). Unlike many artists of his time, Catlin tried to produce accurate pictures of the Native American people and their way of life.

Breaking free

By the 1600s, a terrible trade in human slaves was flourishing. Millions of Africans were captured and sent across the ocean to America and the Caribbean islands. Conditions on the slave ships were appalling and more than one third of the Africans died before they reached their destination. Those who survived were sold as slaves. The slaves were owned by their masters for life, and all their children were also slaves.

Slave music

Most American slaves worked in the southern states of North America on large **plantations**. They had to work very long hours in the fields, growing cotton, tobacco, and sugar. To help keep their spirits up during the long hours of backbreaking work, the slaves often sang songs with powerful rhythms. These songs were known as "**spirituals**".

This photograph shows a slave family, working on a cotton plantation. It was taken in 1860, five years before slavery was made illegal throughout the USA.

Photographs of slaves

Slavery in the southern states of North America was abolished in 1865, and finally ended in the 1880s, but before that time a few early photographers recorded the lives of the slaves. Some moving portraits survive of slave families, dressed in ragged clothes, but looking proud and dignified.

Many of the spirituals told of the harshness of the slaves' lives and expressed their longing to be free. They include such titles as *Sometimes I feel like a motherless child*, *Go down Moses* and *Steal away*. These memorable songs are still sung today.

Sometimes I feel like a motherless child expresses the sadness of slaves cut off from their families and their homeland. *Go down Moses* tells the story of the people of Israel escaping from slavery in Egypt, and also voices the hope that the American slaves will one day be free. *Steal away* is about slaves escaping from their daily suffering – either by dying and going to heaven, or by running away.

Quilts with a message

Slave families had very little free time for creating art, but some women did manage to make quilts. These handmade quilts were more than just works of art. They often included hidden messages about ways to escape from slavery.

The patterns, knots, stitching, and colours all provided instructions about safe routes to freedom. By following these secret routes, slaves could escape from the southern states to the northern states, where slaves could be free. Symbols such as the "north star" or the "flying geese" were also important indications of which routes to follow.

In the 1860s, William Sheppard produced a series of illustrations showing life on a cotton plantation. These prints were reproduced in the weekly magazine *Harper's Bazaar*. Sheppard shows the white plantation farmers watching while the slaves do all the work. However, he makes the slaves' work seem much more pleasant than it really was.

The spirit of revolution

In the 1780s, the ordinary people of France decided they could no longer suffer under the rule of their cruel and extravagant king. They rose up in a bloody rebellion, which became known as the "French Revolution". The French Revolution meant the end of the monarchy in France. It led to the creation of a **republic** – a country run by leaders who were chosen by the people.

The French Revolution marked a new spirit of independence among the ordinary people of Europe. This spirit was reflected in the art of the period. In the 19th century, artists began to paint more images of ordinary people, rather than the **aristocracy**.

They also started painting in a freer and more passionate way, known as the Romantic style.

Image of revolution

The French Revolution caught the imagination of many artists, but the most outstanding image of the conflict was Eugéne Delacroix's *Liberty leading the people*. This famous Romantic work was painted in response to the 1830 revolution in France, over 40 years after the famous 1789 Revolution. It is not intended to be a realistic image of the conflict. Instead it shows the giant female figure of Liberty, holding the French flag in one hand and a gun in the other, leading a group of revolutionaries over a sea of bodies.

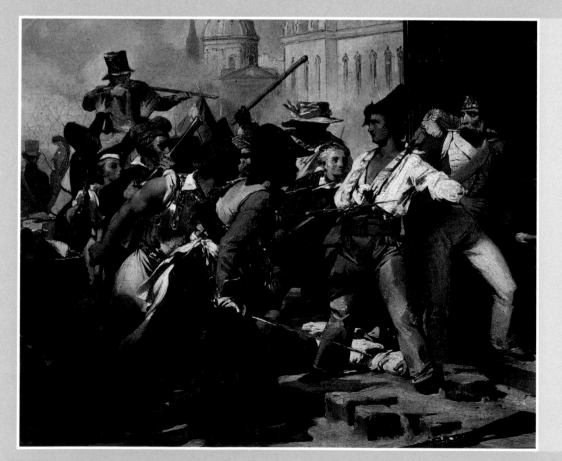

A dramatic scene from the 1830 revolution, painted by Léon Cogniet. Over 50 years after the French Revolution, French citizens took to the streets again in a violent protest against their government. Cogniet's painting captures the defiant spirit of the ordinary people.

The revolutionaries in Delacroix's painting represent a range of social classes. One, dressed in a smart hat and coat, is member of the middle class, while another, in a shirt and beret, is a working class man. A peasant woman kneels at Liberty's feet and a raggedly dressed young boy races after her. The message of the painting is very clear. Liberty is the friend of the ordinary people, and is not on the side of the king and the aristocracy.

The American Revolution

A few years before the French Revolution, the North American **colonies** rebelled against the British king.

In 1776, led by George Washington, they declared independence from Britain and established an independent nation, the United States of America.

Many North American artists produced stirring images of the American Revolution and its leaders. One famous painting by John Trumbull shows the leaders of the colonies signing the **Declaration of Independence**. The group of leaders represent the spirit of the new country of America. Trumbull shows them as modestly dressed, honest, and upstanding men, all sharing power together.

John Trumbull, *The Declaration of Independence, 4 July 1776* (1786–1820). This painting is based on Thomas Jefferson's description of the event (Jefferson is shown here in a red waistcoat). However, Trumbull altered the truth a little to make his picture a stronger statement of American unity. Instead of painting a single figure presenting the declaration, he showed all the colony leaders presenting it together.

A changing world

In 1782, the British engineer James Watt invented the steam engine. Over the next hundred years, this important invention had a dramatic effect on the way people lived all over the world. Steam engines were used to power machines in factories. They were also used in trains and ships. This meant that goods could be made in factories and transported to where they were needed. The industrial society had begun.

Factories and towns

By the 1850s, many people had moved to the towns to find work in the new factories. While the factory owners lived in large, comfortable houses, the workers had to live in very poor areas. These dirty, crowded parts of town were known as slums. People who lived in the slums had very hard lives. They had to work incredibly long hours, and many of them died young.

Life in the towns

Several artists, writers, and photographers recorded life in the 19th-century towns. The British author Charles Dickens produced some heartbreaking stories of poor children in Victorian London. In Dickens' novel *Oliver Twist*, Oliver and his friends have to work as **pickpockets** in order to survive in the city.

Some early photographers recorded life in city slums. One famous picture by an unknown photographer shows a group of slum children standing without smiling, staring out at the camera. One small girl holds a baby in her arms. All of the children wear dirty, tattered clothes, and most of them are barefoot. Photographs like these helped to make the rich aware of the way the poor people lived. Some rich people formed societies to help the poor and tried to get schools and hospitals built in the towns.

Lowry's towns

The untrained artist L. S. Lowry painted the factory towns of northern England. Lowry worked in the first half of the 20th century, when the factories were still very busy. Lowry's distinctive scenes show huge, dark buildings with tall towers belching out smoke into grey skies. Huddled below the factory buildings are the small, red-brick houses of the workers. The streets are filled with the figures of tiny people. Often these figures are shown trudging to work, or heading wearily for home. But if you look closely, there's usually also plenty of fun happening in the city streets.

Lowry's paintings can be looked at in different ways. Are the huge factory buildings menacing and monstrous or are they just friendly and familiar sights? And are his figures trapped unwillingly in their city lives? Or are they part of a close and lively community?

L.S. Lowry *Coming from the mill* (c. 1930). Lowry's painting shows crowds of factory workers pouring out of the gates of a cotton mill. The workers look exhausted after their long day's labour. But there are also children on the street. Are they having fun, or are they also trapped in a world ruled by factories?

The growth of the middle class

By the 1850s, society in the Western world was changing. Between the rich and the poor, there was a growing "middle class". Middle class people had fairly well-paid jobs, such as teaching, working for the government, or owning shops. They had some education and lived in comfortable homes. They also had time and money to spend on leisure.

A different way of life

Two of the things that middle-class people spent their money on were travel and clothes. This was thanks to the railways and factories. The arrival of the railways meant that not just the rich could afford to travel. Middle-class families began to visit the coast, and several seaside resorts grew up. Meanwhile, factories produced very cheap cloth. This meant that middle class people could buy fashionable clothes. The development of better transport also meant women could find out about the latest trends in the rest of Europe.

A new subject for artists

Some artists saw the middle classes as an interesting new subject for art. In particular, a group of French painters called the **Impressionists** concentrated on painting the middle classes (see box). The Impressionists showed smartly dressed people enjoying themselves in parks or restaurants, or on holiday.

The Impressionists

The Impressionists tried to capture this new modern life in their paintings. They were interested in observing people's daily lives, including showing them enjoying pastimes, such as going to the theatre or taking a boat trip. Impressionist artists painted directly in front of their subjects, usually in just one sitting. This meant they had to paint quickly and this gave their pictures a loose quality, filled with energy.

Eugéne Boudin, *Bathers on the Beach at Trouville* (1869). In the foreground, two small children are playing on the sand, but all the adults seem content to sit or stand – simply enjoying being by the sea.

Out and about

Several artists painted people at leisure in Paris. Pierre-Auguste Renoir and Edouard Manet showed life in the city's restaurants and bars, while Georges Seurat pictured people beside the River Seine. In *Sunday on the Island of Grande Jatte*, workers from the factory in the background relax by the water. In a boat, a man wears a top hat, showing he is wealthier than the group with bowler and straw hats on the bank. The woman in the boat is shading herself with a parasol. They can afford to pay someone to row them.

Train travel

Claude Monet and Edouard Manet both showed families travelling by train. Monet's pictures of the Gare Saint Lazare, a busy Paris railway station, convey the excitement of railway travel, as lively passengers with lots of luggage wait for their train. Manet's painting *The Railway* depicts two girls waiting for a train.

Both of them are beautifully dressed, and the older girl has a puppy on her lap and a book in her hand. These are interesting clues to the kind of lives that middle class children enjoyed.

Seaside outings

Manet painted several scenes of couples at the seaside, messing around in boats or sitting on a beach. Meanwhile, Eugéne Boudin produced a series of images of middle class families on holiday by the sea. In Boudin's paintings, some people walk around or look out to sea, while others are seated on upright wooden chairs. Everybody is very smartly dressed – the men wear suits and the women wear long dresses and hats, and carry parasols to shade themselves from the sun. Even the children wear miniature versions of their parents' clothes. To modern eyes, the scene seems rather dull, but a trip to the sea must have been an exciting adventure at the time.

Georges Seurat, *Bathing at Asniéres* (1883–1884). Seurat's painting of bathers shows a less well-off group of people relaxing by the riverside, enjoying themselves after a hard week's work.

Facing poverty

By the start of the 20th century, many people in Europe and America were enjoying a comfortable lifestyle. However, the good times soon came to an end. The First World War plunged Germany into poverty. Then, in the 1930s, many banks and companies failed in North America. This financial crisis was known as the "Great **Depression**". It spread rapidly through America and Europe. During the Depression, money became almost worthless and millions of people lost their homes and jobs. Artists in Europe and America created some powerful images of people coping with poverty and loss.

Suffering in Germany

After the First World War, the city streets of Germany were filled with beggars. A group of artists produced some savage paintings showing the contrast between the greedy rich and the desperate poor. These artists painted in a strong, expressive style that was deliberately intended to shock. They became known as the German **Expressionists**.

One of the leading German Expressionists was George Grosz. In his *Berlin Street Scene*, Grosz shows a wealthy couple completely ignoring a hunched old man who has his hand held out, begging for money. The two rich characters are presented as ugly **caricatures**, while the poor old man in his shabby suit is painted in a much more sympathetic style. In this striking painting, Grosz's anger about society's neglect of the poor is expressed very powerfully.

Berlin Street Scene was painted by George Grosz in the early 1920s. A blind survivor of World War I, selling matches, is being ignored by all the people passing by, who are shown as ugly and corrupt.

Records of the Depression

In North America during the 1930s, several photographers recorded the sufferings of homeless people. In particular, Dorothea Lange produced some moving portraits of **migrant** workers travelling around the country looking for jobs. One of Lange's most famous photographs is *Migrant Mother*. It shows a worn and desperate-looking woman gazing ahead while her three ragged children each bury their heads on her shoulders in despair.

By photographing the mother straight on, Dorothea Lange allows her subject to make a direct appeal for help to the viewer. Even though you cannot help this particular woman, the photograph can make you want to help others.

Henri Cartier-Bresson

In France, the photographer Henri Cartier-Bresson concentrated on the lives of the poor. One of his best-known images shows a small, scruffily dressed young boy returning home from a shop, carrying a bottle under each arm. The boy is clearly not well off but his cheeky optimism shines through the photograph. In this famous image, Cartier-Bresson is celebrating the strength of the human spirit.

This Henri Cartier-Bresson photograph shows a family surviving in a wooden shack on the wasteland at the edge of a city. Why do you think Cartier-Bresson included the blocks of flats in the background?

Social extremes

In the early years of the 20th century, a major revolution took place in Russia. This led to the overthrow of Russia's ruler, the Tsar, and the creation of the Soviet Union. The Soviet Union lasted from 1922 to 1991. It had a new system of government, known as **communism**.

Under the Soviet communist system, all the wealth and land of a country was owned by the state and everyone in the country was forced to work for the state. Even artists and **sculptors** had to create work that reflected communist ideas. Artists were given state projects to work on, and if they created works that criticized the communist system or its leaders, they were banished, imprisoned, or killed.

Soviet art

Sculptors in the Soviet Union produced massive statues of ordinary people at work. These imposing works of art were not intended to be beautiful. Instead, their purpose was to inspire the Soviet people to work as hard as they could for their country.

One of the leading Soviet sculptors was Vera Mukhina. Her sculptures usually show young and muscular men and women dressed in simple peasant clothes. The figures stride proudly forward, holding up their tools. One of the main aims of these imposing figures is to make the communist way of life seem heroic.

Artists in the Soviet period also produced striking posters. Some posters showed labourers in the fields and factories, and others portrayed soldiers and sailors fighting wars. The posters are bold and simple in design, and use just a few strong colours. Like the sculptures, they send out a powerful message that everyone must work hard to make the communist system work.

Vladimirovich Ioganson, *Lenin at the Red Square in Moscow* (1923). This painting by a Soviet artist shows the Communist leader Lenin as an inspiring hero. The square is filled with people eager to hear his words, and the painting is full of red flags waved by communists.

Images of Mao

In the 1940s, China became a communist country. China was ruled for 27 years by Chairman Mao. He controlled all aspects of Chinese life, including art. In particular, Mao encouraged artists to create images of himself. Portraits of Mao were reproduced on giant public posters, but also on stamps, medals, matchboxes, badges, and plates. These images helped to remind the Chinese people that Chairman Mao controlled every aspect of their lives.

Pulling down the statues

By the 1980s, communism was collapsing in Russia and Eastern Europe and in 1991 the Soviet Union came to an end. Since then, most of the statues made during the Soviet period have been pulled down. They are seen as an unwanted reminder of a system that made millions of people suffer.

This poster for the Chinese communist party has the title *Glorious Leader*. It shows a young Chairman Mao surrounded by books and papers. The message sent out by the poster is that Mao is a serious, intelligent man who works hard to find the best way forward for his people. Art used to affect people's political beliefs is known as "propaganda".

Nazi and fascist ideas

In 1933 Adolf Hitler and his **Nazi party** took control of Germany. Hitler believed that the German race was the best and purest in the world, and he wanted to create a vast German Empire. The form of government that Hitler introduced in Germany is known as **fascism**. Under the fascist system, the leader has total power, and can even give orders for some groups of people in his country to be killed.

Fascist art and music

Hitler insisted that German artists should only produce work that glorified the German people and their country. He seized foreign art and banned any art that sent out the "wrong" messages.

During the Nazi period, Fascist artists painted sunny scenes of workers and families set against beautiful German landscapes. They also painted pictures of Nazi solders and military rallies, and the Nazi **swastika** flag often featured clearly in these paintings. The style of these paintings was realistic, but also romantic. They showed a "picture book" image of the German people and their countryside. Hitler hoped that these paintings would inspire the German people to work for his dream of an ideal German way of life.

Hitler also encouraged some German composers. He especially admired the operas of Wagner because they told the stories of courageous German heroes and were full of powerful, stirring tunes.

46

Fascist architecture

Hitler planned to fill German cities with grand new buildings in the fascist style. They would be huge and imposing, with many features from the architecture of Ancient Greece and Rome. Their purpose was to show the power and strength of Germany. However, very few were actually built.

A propaganda poster for the Nazi party created in the mid-1930s. The poster uses the Nazi colours – black, white, and red – and has the slogan, "Germany is free!" The artist has cleverly managed to make it seem as if Hitler and Germany are the same thing, so by supporting Hitler people will be supporting their country.

Another fascist leader, Benito Mussolini, ruled Italy at the same time as Hitler was ruling Germany. Mussolini built many buildings in Rome in the fascist style. Mussolini's buildings are massive and block-like. They are often decorated with huge carved figures, who are shown wrestling, swimming, or working in the fields.

Banning art

The Nazi party banned any art that did not send out the message that the German people were brave, pure, and strong. They especially hated the paintings of the German Expressionists (see page 42) because they showed corrupt and wealthy German people. Hitler hated modern art that showed landscapes in surprising colours. He said that artists who painted like this should not be allowed to be artists because they had something wrong with their eyes.

This gigantic "palazzo" (or palace) was built in Rome for Mussolini in the 1930s. It was intended to be a kind of museum, housing the treasures of Italian fascist culture. The palazzo's massive size, and its series of rounded arches, were deliberately copied from the buildings of Ancient Rome, such as the colosseum. It soon became known as the "square colosseum".

Into the modern world

During the 20th century, society in the West changed very rapidly. By the 1950s, many homes had fridges, washing machines, and vacuum cleaners. At the same time, people began to eat more "convenience" foods. These changes meant that people had far more leisure time than before. In particular, women's lives changed dramatically.

As people had more free time, magazines, television, and cinema all became very popular. Advertising began to play an important part in people's lives. People wanted to buy more and more things for themselves and their homes. All these changes in society were reflected by the artists of the time.

Andy Warhol

The American artist Andy Warhol was fascinated by the way that people lived in the 20th century. He realized that advertising played a very important part in their lives. He also noticed that most people bought very similar **products**.

Andy Warhol produced art that reflected his views on modern society. One of his most famous works is a series of *32 Campbell's Soup Cans*. These painted soup cans are all exactly the same. They can be seen as a comment on the 20th-century way of life, where everybody buys the same **brands**, and eats the same foods.

Perhaps Andy Warhol is also saying that people in the modern world do not vary much. Alternatively, he could be glad of a new era which gives more people greater opportunities.

In the 1960s, Andy Warhol produced a series of "mass-produced" images of stars. This portrait of Marilyn Monroe is one of a series of identical images, each coloured slightly differently, using the style of cheap comic art. The portraits suggest that Marilyn is no longer a human being, but a consumer product created by Hollywood.

David Hockney, *Swimming Pool* (1978–1980). Hockney has produced many images of swimming pools, and most of them are empty like this. The pools represent the pleasures of modern life, but they also show its loneliness and emptiness.

Andy Warhol saw that the **media** had turned Marilyn Monroe into an international superstar. Her image was repeated thousands of times all over the world. She was recognized by her blonde hair and shapely painted lips. Warhol created a portrait that focuses on these characteristics. He did this by obtaining a Polaroid photograph of her wearing flat white make-up. This was then used to make a stencil for a screen print. He could then make as many copies in as many colour combinations as he wished.

Pop Art

Andy Warhol was part of the **Pop Art** movement. Other artists in the movement often used the styles of magazines and comics to show objects or scenes from modern life. In 1956 the British artist

Richard Hamilton created a **collage** called *Just what is it that makes today's homes so different, so appealing?* This shows a modern couple posing in their living room surrounded by all the things they have bought, including a giant tin of ham. Hamilton is asking: Do all these objects really make people happy?

In the 1960s, another British Pop Artist, David Hockney, began a series of paintings of Californian swimming pools. These turquoise pools and cloudless skies present a modern vision of the perfect way to live. However, the scenes are empty and lonely. Hockney seems to raise a series of questions: Where are the people? Is this the way to find happiness? And is there more to life than this?

Society today

Today, society is very different from the way it was 50 years ago. New technology allows many people to communicate with each other very easily. However, at the same time, older social links are breaking down. Many people feel isolated in modern society. There are serious tensions between different social groups, and there is an enormous gap between the rich and the poor. Some contemporary artists have used their art to highlight the problems in our society.

Ordinary lives?

The American artist Duane Hanson, who died in 1996, created life-sized sculptures of ordinary people, whom he thought were neglected by society. Hanson's incredibly lifelike sculptures show overweight builders, tired cleaning women, and bored housewives with shopping trolleys. By placing his figures in art galleries (spaces usually reserved for "fine art"), Hanson celebrates these people as heroes of everyday life.

Another American sculptor, George Segal, also produced sculptures of ordinary people. Segal's pale, anonymous figures are made from plaster casts wrapped in bandages. He shows people riding on buses, waiting in queues, or trudging home wearily from work. In his portraits of faceless, isolated people, Segal highlights the loneliness of modern life.

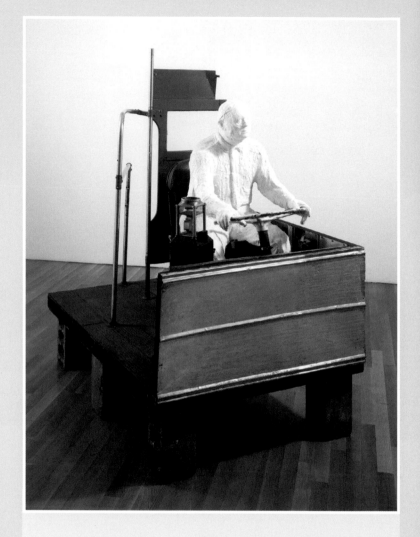

George Segal, *Bus Driver* (c. 1960). Segal's sculpture shows a driver at the wheel of a city bus. The driver looks pale and ghostly against the brutal machinery that he is operating. There is a sense that the bus is controlling the driver rather than the other way around. He is simply filling his role in modern society.

Celebrating outsiders

The British artist Tom Hunter concentrates on the fate of the "outsiders". He has produced some moving photographic portraits of people living on the edge of modern society. One set of works shows a community of squatters, living illegally in empty houses in London. Other works illustrate the lives of a group of travellers, who are constantly forced to move from place to place.

In Hunter's 21st century photographs, people are often arranged to look like those in famous paintings of the past.

By using these techniques, Hunter is making a powerful statement: the lives of modern "outsiders" deserve to be treated with just as much dignity as the subjects of the great masters.

What next?

Our society is changing incredibly rapidly, but there will always be artists to comment on these changes. For thousands of years, artists have been producing images of society. And, whatever happens in the future, we can be sure that artists will continue to put up a mirror to our lives.

Tom Hunter, *Woman Reading a Repossession Order* (1988)
In this beautiful and solemn portrait, a young mother reads the news that she is about to be turned out of her house. The photograph is a commentary on the harshness of modern life. It is also a deliberate echo of Jan Vermeer's famous portrait, *Woman in Blue Reading a Letter*. By copying Vermeer's masterpiece, Hunter is saying that the woman in his portrait deserves to be viewed with as much respect as the subject of a famous painting.

Map and Further reading

GERMANY
HOLLAND
UNITED KINGDOM
RUSSIA
UNITED STATES OF AMERICA
EUROPE
ASIA
FRANCE
ITALY
GREECE
JAPAN
CHINA
SPAIN
Atlantic Ocean
MEXICO
Pacific Ocean
IRAN
AFRICA
Pacific Ocean
SOUTH AMERICA
Indian Ocean
AUSTRALASIA

Map of the world

This map shows you roughly where in the world some key works of art discussed in this book were produced. The countries marked relate to the timeline, opposite.

Further Reading

History in Art series
(Raintree, 2005)

Directions in Art series
(Heinemann Library, 2003)

Art in History series
(Heinemann Library, 2001)

Eyewitness Art: Looking at Paintings, Jude Welton, (Dorling Kindersley, 1994)

Timeline

The dates in this timeline are simply intended to give a rough idea of when works of art were produced.

BCE

c.30,000 Cave painters show hunters chasing animals

c.14,000 Cave painters show hunters and chiefs performing ritual dances

c.2,000 Ancient Egyptian artists start to show farmers, pharaohs, queens, warriors, and slaves.

c.200 Artists in China start painting portraits of their emperors

c.20 Roman artists start to show powerful emperors. Roman artists also show soldiers and generals, craft workers and slaves.

CE

c.520 Byzantine artists portray the Emperor Justinian and the Empress Theodora (modern-day Greece, Turkey, Italy, and Spanish and African Mediterranean coastal areas)

c. 1100s Artists in medieval Europe start to show rulers, nobles, and knights. Medieval artists also show merchants, craft workers, and serfs.

c.1530 Hans Holbein becomes court painter for King Henry VIII of England

c.1550s Pieter Bruegel the Elder starts to paint peasants at work and at play (Belgium)

c.1600s Sculptors in West Africa portray rulers and queen mothers

Artists in India show the Mogul court

c.1650s Jan Vermeer and other Dutch artists paint portraits of servants

1750s Thomas Gainsborough starts work as a portrait painter of the British aristocracy

1806 Jean Auguste Dominique Ingres paints the Emperor Napoleon (France)

1830 Eugéne Delacroix paints *Liberty Leading the People* (France)

1840s George Caleb Bingham starts to paint settlers in North America

1857 Jean-François Millet paints *The Gleaners* (France)

1870s Eugéne Boudin and other French artists paint images of families at the seaside

1880s John Singer Sargent starts to paint leading members of society in North America

1886 Georges Seurat completes *A Sunday on La Grande Jatte* (France)

1920s George Grosz attacks German society through his paintings

Artists in the Soviet Union start to create "communist art" (modern-day Russia)

L.S. Lowry starts to paint life in the factory towns of northern England

1930s Dorothea Lange photographs poor workers in North America

Artists in Germany produce "fascist art"

1960s Andy Warhol produces his works commenting on 20th-century society (USA)

Pop art flourishes

Glossary

Aboriginal people people who have lived in a country for thousands of years, before later settlers arrived

ancestor a family member who lived a long time ago

aristocracy members of the ruling class

brand a particular make of product

brocade a rich fabric with a raised pattern on it. The patterns on brocade are often woven from gold or silver thread.

caricature a humorous picture of someone that exaggerates their features

ceramics objects made from clay

citizens people who live in a city

coat of arms a design in the shape of a shield that is used as the special sign of a family

collage a work of art made by sticking lots of different things onto a surface

colonies settlements created in a foreign land by people who have moved away from their homeland

commission to pay an artist to create a work of art

communism a way of running a country in which the government owns all the land and the factories. Everybody works for the government, and it provides for all the people's needs.

courtiers people who work at court, serving a ruler

Declaration of Independence a document signed in 1776, stating that the American colonies were no longer owned by Britain, but were an independent country

depict to show through a work of art

Depression a time in the 1930s when people in many countries became extremely poor

divine godlike, or connected with God

divine right God-given right

effigies statues of dead people carved on their tombs

embroider to sew patterns or pictures onto cloth

Expressionist a style in art which aims to express the artist's emotions and which uses bold shapes and colours

fascism a way of running a country in which the country's leader has all the power

figurehead someone, like a king or queen, whose role is to represent their country. Figureheads do not usually have much real power.

fresco wall painting

Impressionist a style of painting in which artists try to show the impression that something has on their senses

industrial society a way of life involving factories, vehicles, and machinery

informal casual, and not stiff or posed

Islamic the civilization developed by Muslims, who follow the religion Islam

knight a skilled warrior. In medieval Europe, knights rode on horses

ladies-in-waiting women who look after an important lady, such as a queen

loincloth a simple cloth worn around waist and hips

manuscript a hand-written book

massacre a brutal killing of large numbers of people

media television, cinema, newspapers, and magazines

medieval belonging to the period from approximately 1000 CE to 1450 CE

merchant someone who buys and sells goods

Middle Ages the period of history between approximately 1000 CE and 1450 CE

middle class a class of people in society, who are in between the ruling class and the working class. Teachers and doctors are members of the middle class.

migrant travelling. Migrant workers travel from place to place to find work.

monarch a king or a queen

monarchy the rule of kings or queens

mosaic a picture or pattern made up of tiny pieces of coloured stone or glass

mosque a building where Muslims go to worship and pray

Nazi party a party led by Adolf Hitler, who ruled Germany between 1933 and 1945. The Nazis used force against anyone who disagreed with them.

nobles/nobility members of the ruling class. Lords and barons are members of the nobility.

peasants poor people who have to work on their master's land

pickpockets thieves who help themselves to other people's money

pharaoh an Ancient Egyptian ruler

pioneer someone who travels to wild areas in order to find new places to settle

plantations very large farms

Pop Art a movement in art that reflected the styles used in advertising and the media. Pop Art flourished in the 1960s.

portray to show something or someone through art, music or writing

prehistoric belonging to a time millions of years ago, before history was written down

product something made by a machine

prophet Mohammed the founder of the religion of Islam. Muslims believe that Mohammed was the main prophet (teacher) of God's message.

republic a country run by leaders who are chosen by the people. Republics do not have a king or queen.

rituals a set of actions that are always performed in the same way

sculptor someone who creates a work of art from stone, wood, metal or other materials

serfs poor people who have to work on their master's land.

sophisticated not simple

spiritual a song sung by slaves in the southern states of America

supernatural not belonging to the natural world. Ghosts, spirits, and gods are all supernatural beings.

swastika a symbol used by Hitler's Nazi party

textiles materials or fabrics

Index

Titles in the *Through Artists' Eyes* series include:

Hardback   1 406 20151 0

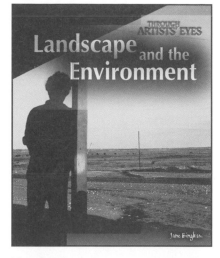

Hardback   1 406 20153 7

Hardback   1 406 20152 9

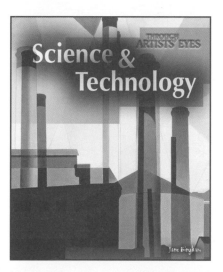

Hardback   1 406 20154 5

Hardback   1 406 20150 2

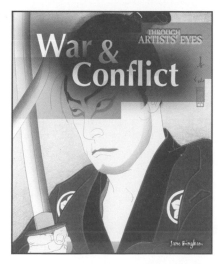

Hardback   1 406 20149 9

Find out about other raintree titles on our website www.raintreelibrary.co.uk